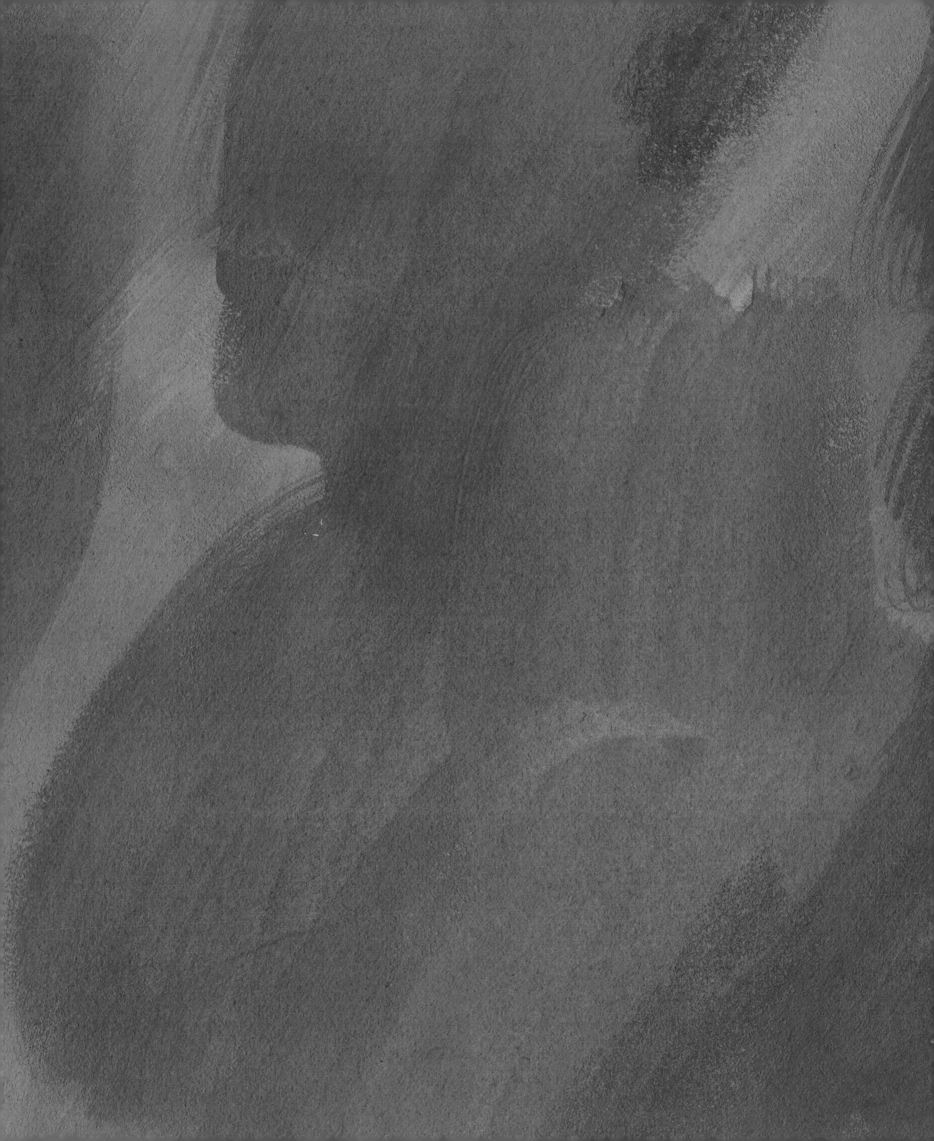

Barefoot Books

AMAZING PLACES

written by **Miralda Colombo**

illustrated by **Beatrice Cerocchi**

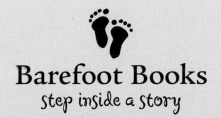

Barefoot Books
step inside a story

Ready to Go?

It's time for your guided tour through fifteen of the world's most remarkable monuments!

Our world is a round globe, but maps are flat. A flat map can't perfectly show where all of the places are on a round globe because things look different on a round surface and on a flat surface. This map shows the globe's round surface on a flat surface.

Tips for Travel

There are incredible sights to see all over the world, whether you travel around the globe or just to the next town. The fifteen landmarks in this book are only a few among countless amazing places on every continent. No matter where your travels take you, remember to come with a curious mind that is ready to learn and grow from trying new things. Speak and act with kindness and respect for the people you meet. And try to leave a place the way you found it, so that others can enjoy it after you.

What's the most amazing place you've ever seen?

Types of Places

Here are some of the places or **monuments** you will find in this book. A monument is a building or piece of art that is important to history, celebrates an event or helps us remember a person.

amphitheatre: an outdoor performance space shaped like a circle, with seats surrounding the stage so everyone has a good view. The Colosseum is an amphitheatre built by the ancient Romans.

castle: a building where nobles or royalty live, usually surrounded by a moat or other protective features. Neuschwanstein Castle was designed to look like older European castles.

cathedral: a type of church run by a bishop. The Sagrada Família is one of the most famous cathedrals in the Roman Catholic religion.

city: a large town. No one lives in the ancient cities of Chichén Itzá, Machu Picchu and Petra anymore, but their buildings still stand. You can visit and imagine what life used to be like there.

mausoleum: a monument or building with a tomb inside. A tomb is where a dead body is buried. The Taj Mahal and Pyramid of Khufu are both mausoleums.

opera house: a type of theatre where operas, ballets and other arts events are performed. The Sydney Opera House is one of the largest in the world.

statue: a piece of art that usually represents a person, animal or mythical being. Statues can be sculpted or carved from rock, metal or other materials. The Moai of Easter Island and *Christ the Redeemer* are statues.

stone circle: an arrangement of tall stones in a circle. These monuments are found across northern Europe, but the most famous is Stonehenge in Great Britain.

temple: a building used for worship or to show respect. In some religions, temples are considered the actual homes of gods or goddesses. The Parthenon and Angkor Wat are temples.

watchtower: a tall structure with openings for guards to look out of for signs of danger. There are many watchtowers all along the Great Wall of China.

Taj Mahal 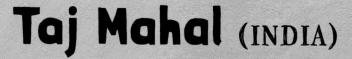 (INDIA)

It sparkles in the sunlight, crowned by its pure white dome. It is not a religious building or an artistic monument — it's the largest mausoleum in the world. Built by order of Mughal ruler Shah Jahan, this palace of marble and semiprecious stones is where the emperor buried his beloved wife, Mumtaz Mahal. Located along the shores of the Yamuna River in Agra, India, the Taj Mahal was completed almost 400 years ago.

Enter and Be Amazed

The impressive entryway is made of red sandstone. Look up and count the twenty-two little cupolas (rounded domes) on top. They are smaller versions of the main dome.

Want to take a selfie? Sit down on this marble bench. The Taj Mahal and the Chahar Bagh Gardens will be behind you. The gardens are divided into four parts by crisscrossing waterways.

Stop and examine the arches at the entryway. The verses of the Koran, the sacred book of the Muslim faith, get gradually larger as they go up the arch so that they seem to stay the same size from where you stand.

Take your shoes off and enter the small room containing the tomb of the princess and the emperor. The raised tombstone is decorated with flowers and quotations from the Koran, promising the joys of paradise.

The Word to Know

The Mughal empire ruled a large area of south Asia from the 1500s to 1800s CE. The first Mughal emperor, or **shah**, was a descendant of the famous warlord Genghis Khan.

Pack Your Bag

- A pair of socks. You must take off your shoes to enter the Taj Mahal, but in winter the marble is freezing!
- A book by Rabindranath Tagore, the Indian poet who wrote, "The Taj Mahal rises above the banks of the river like a solitary tear suspended on the cheek of time."

Look Up Close

The building's four minarets (narrow towers) lean slightly outwards. Some archaeologists think they were designed that way so that they wouldn't fall onto the main building in case of an earthquake.

Meet Shah Jahan

When Mughal Prince Khurram was a teenager, his parents made a deal with the parents of a young woman named Arjumand. The parents decided that their children would get engaged. Even though they were young, the prince fell passionately in love with Arjumand. When he became Shah Jahan, she was called Mumtaz Mahal, which means "light of the palace." She died giving birth to her fourteenth child in 1631. Shah Jahan promised to satisfy the last wish of his beloved: to never forget her.

Tell Me a Story

Shah Jahan was the emperor who paid for the Taj Mahal. He was overcome with grief after the death of his beloved wife, Mumtaz Mahal. He didn't eat for eight days. Then he gathered artists and builders to begin the monument, which took 16 years to complete. A few years later, Shah Jahan became ill and his son took power. When Shah Jahan died, he was also buried in the Taj Mahal.

Wow!

If you sit down in the gardens in front of the Taj Mahal, you'll discover that the marble palace never looks the same. Its appearance changes depending on the hour of the day and the mood of the sky: pink in the morning, white by day, intense red at dusk and golden beneath the moon.

Pyramid of Khufu (EGYPT)

There are over one hundred pyramids in Egypt, but the most famous ones are located in the city of Giza. The biggest is the 4,500-year-old Pyramid of Khufu, the only one of the Seven Wonders of the Ancient World that still stands. Its stone blocks weigh an estimated 5.4 million tonnes (6 million tons), but that's not the only incredible thing about it. The Pyramid of Khufu is also almost geometrically perfect because all of its sides are nearly the same size. It was the mausoleum of a leader called a pharaoh, whom the ancient Egyptians believed was chosen by the gods.

Enter and Be Amazed

You'll find three main pyramids at Giza: the Pyramid of Khufu, the Pyramid of Khafre and the smallest of the three, the Pyramid of Menkaure.

Take a deep breath and enter the Pyramid of Khufu. Don't get scared! The climb through the narrow, dark corridors doesn't take long.

Cross the Grand Gallery, which is 47 m (154 ft) long, and arrive at Pharaoh Khufu's burial chamber. Inside, there is only an empty coffin made of granite, called a sarcophagus — Khufu's body has never been found.

Next to the Pyramid, discover a giant ship in its own museum. It is 44 m (144 ft) long and was buried here around the same time as Pharaoh Khufu, more than 4,500 years ago.

The Word to Know

The Ancient Egyptians wrote using symbols called **hieroglyphs** that were carved or painted on walls. Hieroglyphs represent objects, animals, people or actions. Each one has its own sound — like "mr" (pronounced "mehr"), which means "pyramid" and looks like this: △

Pack Your Bag

- A keffiyeh, the traditional Arab head covering that protects people from sunburns.
- While you're here, see if you can find a cartouche — an oval-shaped hieroglyph holding a pharaoh's name. Which symbols or hieroglyphs would represent your name?

Tell Me a Story

When Pharaoh Khufu was the ruler of Egypt, he was the most powerful person in the whole country. Historians have learned about him from hieroglyphs, artifacts and other records from ancient Egyptian and Greek writers. Most experts agree that when he became pharaoh, he ordered the construction of the Pyramid of Khufu as the final resting place for his body after death. They think his body was mummified — preserved with minerals and oils and wrapped in linen bandages. Unfortunately, robbers probably stole his remains before archaeologists could find them.

Wow!

Imagine how the Pyramid of Khufu must have looked 4,500 years ago. It used to be entirely covered in smooth slabs of white limestone (except for the top, which some think was gold). It must have looked like a huge mirror in the middle of the desert that reflected the light of the sun.

Meet the Sphinx

The Sphinx is an enormous statue with a lion's body and a human's head. The ancient Egyptians believed it protected the tombs and the pharaohs buried there. It was sculpted from a huge single block of stone 20 m (66 ft) high and 73 m (240 ft) long. The lion was a powerful figure in ancient Egypt; the warrior goddess Sekhmet appears in many statues as a woman with a lion's head.

Look Up Close

The Pyramid of Khufu resembles a gigantic tent. Originally 147 m (481 ft) high, it was the tallest building in the world for more than 3,000 years. It is as tall as a modern skyscraper and is even visible from space! To build it, more than 20,000 workers stacked millions of extremely heavy stone blocks. We know that the workers carried them using wooden sleighs that they pulled through the desert sand, but it's still a mystery how they lifted these massive blocks to the top of the pyramid.

Great Wall of China (CHINA)

The Great Wall of China is the longest and highest wall built in human history. According to one Chinese saying, "We can't be heroes until we have reached the Great Wall," which means that overcoming obstacles makes you brave. Discover the challenges of climbing the Great Wall of China and listen to stories of the warriors who defended themselves from the watchtowers here. Imagine the millions of workers who built the wall over a period of 2,000 years. The wall has many bends and curves, but if it were laid out straight, it would reach more than halfway around the globe.

Enter and Be Amazed

You can't walk its full length in one day or even one month, so you'll have to choose just part of the wall to explore. Avoid the most crowded section at Badaling, near Beijing.

If you want to pretend you are a soldier on guard duty in a watchtower, the best place is the Mutianyu section of the wall. Mutianyu means "the valley of those who admire the fields." Prepare for a steep climb.

Choose one of the watchtowers and look out at the land below you. The Mongolian army, led by the terrible Genghis Khan, would have tried to arrive when you least expected it!

Going back down the valley? If you're not scared of speed, hop on a bobsled and ride down a track. Ready, set, go!

The Word to Know

The Chinese call the Wall "Wanli Changcheng" ("Ten-Thousand-League Wall"). A **league** is a way of measuring distance. Ten thousand leagues is about 5,000 km (3,107 mi). This isn't an exact measurement — it's just a nickname that means the wall is extremely long!

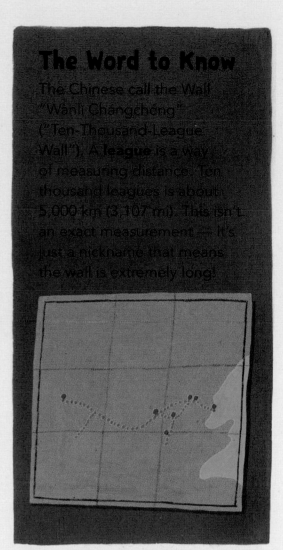

Pack Your Bag

- The perfect hiking outfit: boots, poles, a hoodie and a water bottle. Walking the Wall is tiring!

- How will you remember your adventure? Have your name engraved on a medallion from the Wall.

Meet Qin Shi Huang

Born Ying Zheng, he was only a young boy when he became Qin Shi Huang, or the first emperor of the state of Qin. He dreamed of conquering all of China, which was divided into many states. In 221 BCE, his dream came true and he declared himself the first Chinese emperor. Qin Shi Huang was afraid of two things: his enemies and death. He ordered the construction of a great defensive wall connecting some walls that already existed. The Wall also protected his enormous tomb, which was built under a hill and contained thousands of life-sized warrior statues made of terracotta, a type of clay.

Tell Me a Story

From the lookout tower, the imperial guard shouted the alarm: Here come the invaders! Guards also sent smoke signals by burning wolf droppings; the fires made thick columns of smoke. Five columns of smoke meant that 5,000 enemy soldiers were on their way.

Look Up Close

Built from earth, stone, brick and local materials, the Wall stands 14 m (46 ft) tall at its highest point. The outside is covered in smooth stone to stop enemies from climbing it. At the top are sheltered walkways where four horses could fit side by side and small forts for food and weapons. There are also watchtowers all along the Wall.

Wow!

The Wall twists and turns like a terrible stone serpent, so long that you never see the end of it. The great length of the Wall means that it is difficult to measure. One early estimate was 8,851 km (5,500 mi), but according to recent studies, the total length is 21,196 km (13,171 mi).

Moai (EASTER ISLAND)

The volcanic Easter Island, located in the middle of the Pacific Ocean, was named Rapa Nui by the first Indigenous people who lived there. Almost 900 gigantic statues are scattered around the island, many placed on large stone platforms called ahu. Historians believe the statues represent the ancestors (early relatives) of the people who first lived on the island. These special statues are called moai, and their stone heads have watched over Rapa Nui and its people for many hundreds of years.

Enter and Be Amazed

Rapa Nui is surrounded by the Pacific Ocean. The island is 3,700 km (2,299 mi) from the closest country, Chile. From Rapa Nui, you have a spectacular view of the sea and the stars.

A very long time ago, three volcanoes called Rano Kau, Terevaka and Poike erupted and created this island. On a bicycle, you can journey from the village of Hanga Roa to the volcano Rano Kau.

Before the statues were moved, sculptors made them in the crater of the volcano Rano Raraku. Look inside and you will see more than 400 abandoned statues, only partly finished by the ancient sculptors.

Turn towards the ocean to take a photo of the fifteen moai of Ahu Tongariki, a line of statues with their backs to the sea. In 1960, a massive ocean wave called a tsunami broke the statues, but experts fixed them.

Pack Your Bag

- Boots, which will come in handy as you hike between moai.

- If you bring a compass to find your way around, beware! Some of the rocks here contain so much iron that the compass magnet might not work properly.

The Word to Know

This island is known as **Rapa Nui**, meaning "big Rapa." Rapa is a smaller island nearby. Rapa Nui's Western name, Easter Island, comes from the Dutch explorer Jacob Roggeveen, who arrived there on Easter Day.

Meet the Rapa Nui People

The first people who lived on the island arrived in ships from other places in Polynesia, an area of the southern Pacific Ocean containing more than 1,000 islands. According to Rapa Nui people today, these original islanders brought wooden tablets with writing on them called rongorongo. They used shark teeth and a type of rock called obsidian to cut marks into the tablets. No one has been able to translate the tablets, and they are now in museums and private collections around the world.

Tell Me a Story

When British explorers visited the island, they didn't see many trees, so they thought that the islanders had cut them down. But modern historians believe that rats came to Rapa Nui on the boats of the first settlers and ate tree seeds and sprouts, which made trees stop growing there. Whatever the reason may be, the statues seem even more impressive without tall trees nearby.

Wow!

The moai are so immense that it's hard to imagine how anyone was able to move them from the volcano's crater, where they were carved, to the places where they stand today. Experts think that clever and determined islanders pulled them using a system of ropes. At some point, though, they stopped building and moving moai. Most of the statues remain unfinished.

Look Up Close

The most colossal statue is called Paro, which boasts a height of 10 m (33 ft) and a weight of 73 tonnes (80 tons). That's about as heavy as twenty elephants! Some of the statues wear red "hats" made of red volcanic rock. The moai were sculpted from soft volcanic rock that is slowly crumbling because of wind, rain and temperature changes.

Sagrada Família (SPAIN)

The Sagrada Família of Barcelona, Spain, is a church different from any other in the Roman Catholic religion. The decorated outside walls, called facades, reflect important moments in the life of Jesus Christ, while the inside structure feels like a forest with trunks, branches and leaves made of stone. The most incredible part, though, is that the cathedral is still an active construction site. The work has continued for well over 100 years, thanks to donations from the church's congregation.

Enter and Be Amazed

Its grand towers make the Sagrada Família the tallest church in Barcelona. When finished, its central tower will be just slightly shorter than the nearby Montjuïc mountain. The architect, Antoni Gaudí, did not want it to rise higher than something he believed was created by God.

Even before the base of the church was finished, Gaudí completed the Nativity facade, the scene that shows the birth of Jesus. Its beauty, he thought, would motivate builders to get the rest of the cathedral done.

Look at the numbers in the square on the door of the Passion facade, which is the scene that tells the story of Easter. Try to add the numbers in each row and column. The result is always 33, the age Jesus was when he died.

1	14	14	4
11	7	6	9
8	10	10	5
13	2	3	15

Did you know that Gaudí never abandoned his amazing creation? If you go beyond the forest of columns, you will find his tomb in an underground room called a crypt.

The Word to Know

The Sagrada Família is funded by donations from Roman Catholic **patrons**, people who give money to projects they support. Visitors and people who live in Barcelona also donate to it.

Pack Your Bag

- Swimming gear and sunglasses. After a long visit to the Sagrada, there's nothing better than a dip at a nearby beach.

- Markers and an activity book, a fun way to get to know Gaudí's creations. Fill in the patterns of his palaces, parks and grand cathedral.

Tell Me a Story

Josep María Bocabella owned a bookstore in Barcelona, but in 1861 he took a trip to Rome and became inspired by images he saw there of the Christian holy family: Jesus, Mary and Joseph. He started a spiritual group for other people who felt the same way and they began to raise money for the construction of a church. On March 19, 1882, the group gathered for the feast of Saint Joseph and Bocabella laid the first stone of the Sagrada Família.

Look Up Close

Once it is finished, the Sagrada Família will be the tallest cathedral in the world at a towering 172.5 m (566 ft). The central tower will be topped with a large cross, a holy symbol of Jesus in the Christian and Roman Catholic religions. Once complete, the basilica will have three grand facades and eighteen towers. The towers are each dedicated to important Christian figures. The tallest one represents Jesus Christ.

Meet Antoni Gaudí

Born in the province of Catalonia, Spain, Antoni Gaudí is famous for his imaginative architecture. He liked to build houses with walls featuring battles between dragons and knights, balconies that looked like the mouths of ferocious beasts and parks where stone salamanders appear to climb. Because Gaudí spent almost all of his time working on the Sagrada Família during the last fifteen years of his life, many people called him "the architect of God."

Wow!

What happens when art imitates nature? Something extraordinary like the Sagrada is born. Here, the towers resemble a magical sandcastle, the inside columns look like trees in a stone forest and the shapes of the stairways are like big snails. Because of an illness, Gaudí could not run and play as much as other children when he was young. Instead, he watched flowers, animals and trees for hours. He believed nature was the best art.

Chichén Itzá (MEXICO)

For centuries upon centuries, the jungle has guarded the ruins of Chichén Itzá, a little like the forest that surrounded Sleeping Beauty's kingdom. Chichén Itzá is a city built thousands of years ago by the Itzá, one of the Maya peoples who lived in what is now Mexico. Here you can explore the pyramid-shaped Temple of Kukulkan, the enormous Great Ball Court and the striking Temple of the Warriors. There is even an ancient astronomical observatory, which is a place to study the sun, moon, planets and stars.

Enter and Be Amazed

Leave the emerald forest behind you and enter the ancient Maya city. Stop at the Temple of Kukulkan (a Maya serpent god) in the middle of the city.

At 30 m (98 ft) high, the Temple will tower high above you. Its Four Stairs are guarded by carvings of fierce, feathered serpents with wide-open mouths.

The quetzal is a beautiful bird that was sacred to the ancient Maya and still exists today. At the bottom of the staircase, clap your hands. The sound echoes off every step and makes the birdlike "chirping" you hear.

Inside the Temple of Kukulkan, like a set of nesting dolls, there are two smaller, hidden pyramids. They might have once contained thrones, statues and places for religious rituals.

Wow!

The spring and autumn equinoxes are the two days of the year when day and night are exactly the same length. On these days, the angle of the sun reveals something special on the Temple's staircase. The sunlight connects the head of the snake carved into the bottom of the staircase with its tail, carved all the way at the top. This makes it look like a massive golden-feathered serpent is slithering down the stairs.

Pack Your Bag

- A sombrero, a traditional Mexican hat — it is cone-shaped with a wide brim.

- The recipe for a cup of hot chocolate like Maya kings used to drink it: powdered cocoa, water and hot chili pepper.

Look Up Close

Imagine going back in time and living in Chichén Itzá, near the sacred underground pools of water that gave the city its name — Chichén Itzá means "at the edge of Itzá's well." Near the Temple of Kukulkan, explore big plazas, a market and fields for the ball game called pokolpok. Look around and between the sculpted columns of the Temple of the Warriors. Finally, peek into the Observatory, called El Caracol or "the Snail" because of its spiral staircase. Here, the Maya used stone basins filled with water to see the stars and planets and to set their calendar.

Tell Me a Story

The fields for the ball game called pokolpok are surrounded by slanting walls 12 m (39 ft) high and decorated with carved serpents. Seven players on each team had to hit a rubber ball heavier than a watermelon using only their knees, sides and elbows. The game represented the war between the gods and the dark forces; the ball was the sun. Versions of this game are still played today.

The Word to Know

In the Yucatec Mayan language, **Kukulkan** means "feathered serpent." Legend says that Kukulkan was a hero and a god who taught his knowledge to the Maya before disappearing into the ocean.

Meet the Maya

The Maya people have lived in Central America for 3,500 years. Maya tradition says that humans are shaped from sacred maize (corn, their most important crop). The ancient Maya worshipped Kukulkan and Chaac, the god of rain. Their astronomers and mathematicians developed a solar calendar similar to the one we use today, and they were the first people to use the number zero. They also invented xocoatl, or hot chocolate.

Colosseum (ITALY)

The Colosseum is the most famous open-air stadium in the world, also known as an amphitheatre. Roman emperors entertained their people here for hundreds of years. The Colosseum hosted everything from plays and concerts to ferocious fights between animals and people. It is astonishing both because of its enormous size and its nearly 2,000 years of history. The Roman poet Martial visited it when it was completed in the year 80 CE. He wrote that it was the most incredible thing humans had ever created. Would you agree with him?

Enter and Be Amazed

It's not just the building that's impressive, but also all the things that happened inside it. Imagine people gathered here for entertainment thousands of years ago. Start exploring underground, and then make your way to the highest seats.

Discover the amphitheatre's two underground floors. Follow the tunnels and pretend you are a gladiator, someone trained to fight against other people.

Do you hear the shouts of the crowd and the terrible roaring of the lions? Sixty sets of platforms and ropes worked as elevators to bring animals into the arena.

Now look up. At the highest level of the amphitheatre, 300 ropes held the eighty triangular panels of a rooflike covering. This protected people from the scorching sun.

Wow!

Would you like to witness a battle between ships at sea, like the ones the Romans fought against the Egyptians? In the early years of the Colosseum, the Romans flooded the lowest levels with water so that ships could float on top. Then Roman prisoners were forced to act out famous naval battles in shows called naumachia.

Pack Your Bag

- While you are here, pick up a toy helmet, sword and shield to bring Roman history to life.

- A flashlight, so you can visit the Colosseum at night, if you visit in the summer.

Meet the Gladiators

They were the fighters of ancient Rome, who tested their strength with each other and against captured beasts. Often they were prisoners from Roman wars, slaves or criminals, but sometimes free Romans took the oath of the gladiators and signed up for special fighting schools. A popular myth says that Colosseum crowds got to decide the fate of gladiators who lost a fight. If the audience closed their thumbs into fists, they would be saved, but if the audience pointed their thumbs down, the gladiators would be killed.

Tell Me a Story

In the beginning, the Colosseum was called the Flavian Amphitheatre after the emperors of the time. How did it become the Colosseum? Many think the name comes from the Latin word "colossus" meaning "giant statue," which was originally used to describe a big sculpture of the emperor Nero that stood nearby. That statue was eventually destroyed, but the nickname stuck. The Amphitheatre became "the Colossal," the Colosseum.

Look Up Close

The word "amphitheatre" comes from the ancient Greek words that mean it has a viewing area on both sides: "amphi," meaning "on both sides," and "theatron," meaning "viewing area." The Colosseum's oval viewing area was divided into sections that separated people by how important and rich they were. The emperor and his family had a special box near the bottom with the best view. Senators (lawmakers and advisors to the emperor) in white robes also sat in the closest ring of seats. Common people had to stand at the top, furthest away from the action. Rich people and common people even used different entrances. The Colosseum's many levels were made from different types of limestone.

The Word to Know

Roman poet Juvenal used the phrase **"panem et circenses"** ("bread and circuses") to describe a problem he saw in Rome. He meant that Roman emperors kept people distracted with food and entertainment so that they wouldn't pay attention to politics.

Machu Picchu (PERU)

This breathtaking city high up in the mountains was built by the Inca people nearly 600 years ago. The mighty Inca Empire was the largest civilization in the Americas (North and South America) before European colonizers invaded. It stretched over lands that are now parts of Peru, Ecuador, Bolivia, Argentina, Chile and Colombia. Spanish soldiers, known as conquistadors, destroyed most of the Inca Empire, but it seems that they never found Machu Picchu. The remaining visible buildings are incredible, but possibly even more impressive are the foundations beneath them, which were built to drain heavy rainfall during Machu Picchu's wet season.

Enter and Be Amazed

Make the climb! Retrace the footsteps of the Incas who lived here. This trail, which was part of the Inca road system, goes through two mountain passes over 3,962 m (13,000 ft) high. Make sure you take it easy, or the heights might make you dizzy.

At the entrance to the city, don't miss the chance to take a selfie — and don't be surprised if a llama pops into your photo!

Feeling spiritual? Stop at the Temple of the Sun. Here, Inca people could look at the sky and worship the sun god, Inti. The two windows framed the sunrise during the summer and winter solstices (the longest and shortest days of the year).

Next, head to the Temple of the Moon. You will find it in a natural cave on the side of the mountain overlooking Machu Picchu. It might once have held ceremonial mummies (preserved dead bodies).

The Word to Know

Quechua: the Spanish version of the Indigenous word "qheswa," meaning "valley." Quechua peoples are direct descendants of the Incas, and many still live near South America's Andes mountains.

Pack Your Bag

- Hiking poles and a water bottle. You will be doing a lot of walking at Machu Picchu!

- A pan flute. Do you have any breath left? Try this bamboo instrument. Holding the longest tubes with your right hand and the shortest with your left, breathe into the tubes.

Meet the Incas

The Incas believed that they were descendants of Inti, the sun god. The first king of the Incas, Manco Cápac, was said to be Inti's son. The Inca people were both farmers and warriors. They grew maize (corn) and potatoes, raised llamas and alpacas and built a network of roads that extended through their whole empire. They sent messages and kept records using knotted strings called quipu. Different combinations of knots in various positions on the strings stood for particular numbers and words.

Tell Me a Story

One of the most beautiful and mysterious places in Machu Picchu is Intihuatana, or "the hitching post of the sun." This stone might have been a sundial, which is a type of clock that uses the shadows cast by the sun. In the middle of the day on the equinoxes (the two days of the year when day and night are exactly the same length), it shines directly above the point of Intihuatana and casts almost no shadow.

Look Up Close

The Incas built their city on a cliff 2,430 m (7,972 ft) high. Walls protected the buildings and divided the ground into terraces, which were flat areas cut into the side of a hill used to grow crops. The city was split into a farming area and a living area, where there were more than 200 buildings: temples, altars, houses, fountains, watchtowers and a solar observatory (place to watch the sun). People lived higher or lower in the living zone depending on how rich and important they were.

Wow!

How has a city survived for nearly 600 years in a place where earthquakes happen so often? The buildings contain thousands of stones that were each cut and shaped by hand. The Incas fit them together so perfectly that you can't even get a sheet of paper in between them. When earthquakes happen, the stones shake but fall right back into place — as if they are dancing.

Neuschwanstein Castle (GERMANY)

Neuschwanstein looks like an enchanted castle from a fairy tale! In an area of southern Germany known as Bavaria, it is surrounded by green forests, peaceful lakes and moody mountains. It is one of the most visited castles in the world. The white building looks almost like it is growing out of the rocky cliffs nearby. It was built in the late 1800s for King Ludwig II, and the castle's name means "New Swan Stone" in German, after a story the king loved.

Enter and Be Amazed

You've received an invitation to the court! Ride in your carriage across Marie's Bridge, named after King Ludwig II's mother. Don't be afraid of the height — just admire the Bavarian Alps, the dense forest and the Pöllat river below you.

Swans, swans and more swans! Even the sink in the king's bedroom features a swan. King Ludwig II's most-loved story was about a hero named Lohengrin, known as the Swan Knight.

Check out the Throne Hall. The ceiling is 13 m (43 ft) high and the entire room is decorated in gold and blue. It is the grandest room in the castle, although another room called the Hall of Singers is even larger.

How did Ludwig pass his days? He enjoyed listening to the music of the German composer Richard Wagner.

The Word to Know

Neuschwanstein Castle was inspired by the architecture of the **medieval** period in Europe, also known as the Middle Ages (500 to 1500 CE). Buildings in this style often have pointed towers and round arches. They remind people of fairy tales and stories about brave German knights.

Pack Your Bag

- A map of Romantic Road in Bavaria, so you don't miss a single castle. Dream of princesses and knights in medieval German tales, just like Ludwig did!

- A puzzle of the castle. How will you create Neuschwanstein's magic at home? By putting together thousands of puzzle pieces in its image!

Look Up Close

On top of a cliff 3,035 ft (925 m) high, surrounded by forests, Neuschwanstein stands out with its white stone walls, round columns and dark metal roofs. Architects, builders and artists created a castle inspired by the traditional stories of the Middle Ages that Ludwig loved so much. The construction went on for seventeen years (it was supposed to take three) and only about fifteen rooms were finished out of the 200 that were planned. The castle had all the most modern technology of the time: running water, flushing toilets, telephone lines and an air-heating system.

Wow!

What does Neuschwanstein remind you of? Walt Disney used this castle as a model for his movies and even for the castles at the entrances of his theme parks. That's why it looks like the castles where Cinderella danced and where Sleeping Beauty's prince woke her up.

Meet King Ludwig II

Ludwig became the king of Bavaria at a young age. Soon after, Bavaria lost a war against Prussia (a German state) and then became part of Germany, so he no longer had complete control over his kingdom. Instead, he used his wealth to build castles and palaces where he could imagine himself as a great ruler.

Tell Me a Story

Ludwig loved Wagner's opera *Lohengrin*. Once upon a time, a young duke named Gottfried disappeared, and his guard accused his sister Elsa of killing him. She prayed for help and a swan appeared with a knight. The knight made Elsa promise never to ask his name. She agreed, so the knight fought the guard and won. Elsa married the knight, but could not resist asking his name. He told her that his name was Lohengrin, and then he left her, because she had broken her promise. In the end, it turned out that the swan who had brought Lohengrin to help Elsa was really her brother Gottfried, who had been transformed by a witch.

Petra (JORDAN)

It's best to arrive early — just after dawn — to see the ancient city of Petra, located in the country now known as Jordan. You will enter through the Siq (meaning "the shaft"), a tall and narrow natural gorge in the sandstone rock. At the end of the Siq, you will find Al-Khazneh, the most famous structure in the city. It began as a natural formation of sandstone and was later carved into a breathtaking facade by the Nabatean people who lived here. Wind, sand and human activity have gradually worn away many of its beautiful details, but it is still a magical place.

Enter and Be Amazed

In Arabic, إِفْتَح يَا سِمسِم (Iftah yā simsim!) means "Open, sesame!" — the famous command from the story of Ali Baba and the forty thieves. Try saying it yourself before you look into the opening of the Siq.

Walk or ride a camel along the path. Some sections are so narrow that if you spread your arms, your hands would brush against the walls. In other places, though, the path widens enough that you can see sunlight on the rocks.

Here is Al-Khazneh, which means "the treasury." One legend says that an Egyptian pharaoh buried his treasure in a container at the top. Point your camera right at it — click!

In the film *Indiana Jones and the Last Crusade*, Indiana Jones stops here to admire the facade. It is guarded by statues of two characters from ancient Greek and Roman mythology named Castor and Pollux.

Wow!

Petra is formed from an amazing rock: sandstone, which is made from grains of desert sand that have been transported by wind and water. This soft rock has an incredible ability: It seems to change its appearance throughout the day depending on the light. From dawn to dusk, it can go from pink to red, or even white and yellow with stripes of blue and black. It has a variety of shades because of the many different types of sand grains inside it.

Pack Your Bag

- A hat, hiking boots and light clothing to protect you from the bright sun. Don't forget a camera!

- Books to read about Arab cultures, the ancient Nabateans and the modern Bedouin people of Petra.

Look Up Close

Skilled Nabateans carved detailed facades, statues, archways, walls and pools to gather water out of sandstone. Archaeologists have identified more than 800 such caves sculpted in cliffsides. An impressive system of tunnels helped Petra's 30,000 residents save rainwater to use during the desert's dry seasons. A temple called Qasr al-Bint has wooden beams inside it, too, which experts think helped it survive earthquakes. Most of Petra's ancient buildings are still underground, untouched by modern tourists.

Tell Me a Story

Originally, the Nabateans lived in the Arabian Desert as nomads, which means they moved around from place to place instead of having one single home. They traded with many peoples, including Romans and Greeks, sharing precious metals and spices. Petra was such a convenient location for trading that the Nabateans founded their capital there as a hub for merchants who moved between the West and the East.

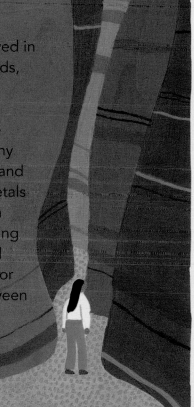

Meet Johann Ludwig Burckhardt

After almost 1,000 years as a successful city, Petra suffered a massive earthquake in the year 363 CE and much of it was destroyed. In 1812, a Swiss man named Johann Ludwig Burckhardt found his way there. He was working as an explorer for a British company that wanted him to travel through Africa. He learned Arabic so he could go through the Arabian Desert. He hired a guide to take him to Cairo, Egypt, and stopped at some interesting ruins along the way. The guide took him to Petra, making Johann the first European to see it in a very long time.

The Word to Know

Because of the variations in sandstone, the Nabateans called their city **Raqmu**, meaning "prismatic," or including the many shades of the rainbow. The name "Petra" comes from the Greek word for "stone."

Parthenon (GREECE)

The Parthenon is a temple that celebrates Athena, the Greek goddess of wisdom. It is located in the city of Athens, Greece, where it rises up from a rocky hill called the Acropolis. Athena was sometimes called "Athena Parthenos," meaning "Athena the maiden," because she never married. The Parthenon is named after her. The architects who built it used a mathematical equation to make the shapes of the building elegant and beautiful.

Enter and Be Amazed

Climb up to the Acropolis, the highest part of the city. Imagine looking at it about 2,500 years ago, admiring its incredible palaces and temples. No Greek city was more beautiful than Athens.

In 447 BCE, General Pericles announced a plan to build many great buildings on the Acropolis to show the glory of Athens — in particular, to outshine its enemies, Sparta and Persia.

Around the top of the Parthenon is a decorated band with ninety-two sculptures in square panels. These sculptures show both historical and mythological events featuring animals and humans.

Inside the Parthenon, there was once a massive statue of Athena made from gold and ivory. It was so large that the sculptor, named Phidias, used more than 1,000 kg (2,205 lbs) of gold for her shield and clothing.

Pack Your Bag

- A sketchbook, so you can draw the shapes of the Parthenon and see if you can figure out its geometry!

- An audiobook of Greek myths. Listen to the stories that inspired the carvings and decorations you see on the Parthenon.

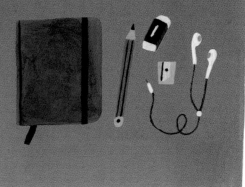

Meet Athena

Legend says that Zeus, the king of the Greek gods, once suffered from a terrible headache. He was in so much pain that he asked another god to split open his head with an axe. Out of his skull came Athena, who was more intelligent than any other god. She became the goddess of all things associated with cleverness and wisdom, from winning wars to keeping peace.

Tell Me a Story

According to Greek mythology, when Athens was first built, two gods had a competition for the right to give it a name: Athena, the goddess of wisdom, and Poseidon, the god of the sea. Poseidon threw his three-pointed spear against a rock and out came a creature no one had ever seen before: a horse. Athena struck the earth with her spear and a silver-leaved tree was born, capable of healing wounds and bringing peace: the olive tree. Athena won and the city was named after her.

Look Up Close

From above, the Parthenon looks like a rectangle. It is raised on a base called a pedestal with three steps, and its sides are made of columns: eight at the front and seventeen along the sides. The temple is magnificently decorated. Inside is the main inner room and the house of the goddess Athena, which was open only to priests. Outside, carvings show stories about wisdom winning over violence. The people and animals are so well-sculpted that they almost seem alive.

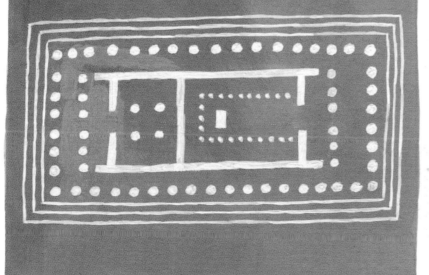

Wow!

The clever artist Phidias took inspiration from nature in his design of the Parthenon. He observed the sizes, shapes and patterns he saw in certain plants and animals. These patterns are called natural geometry. Phidias used natural geometry in his designs to make the temple look beautiful. For example, the columns all lean slightly towards the middle of the building, so that it looks more stable — otherwise, from far away, it would seem like it was about to fall.

The Word to Know

The outside columns of the Parthenon are a little bit wider at the bottom and their square tops are plain rather than decorated. This is called the **Doric** style and is the oldest style of Greek architecture.

Christ the Redeemer (BRAZIL)

This statue stands like a gigantic guardian angel on top of Mount Corcovado, which roughly translates from Brazilian Portuguese as "hunchback mountain." This is the highest point in Rio de Janeiro. More than 70 percent of Rio's citizens are Christian, and some of them say that in the week God spent creating the world, he took two whole days to make Rio. Maybe this is why they decided to celebrate Rio de Janeiro with *Cristo Redentor* or *Christ the Redeemer*, a statue of Jesus Christ that is 38 m (125 ft) tall and weighs 1,039 tonnes (1,145 tons). It has stood watching over all of Rio, surrounded by blue sky and green forest, since it was built in 1931.

Enter and Be Amazed

The first trip of the Trem do Corcovado was in 1884. This little red train goes all the way to the top of the mountain. At first, it was steam-powered, but today it is electric. Sit on the left side of the train to get the best view.

Climb the 222 steps to see *Christ the Redeemer* up close. The plaque on the pedestal is dedicated to Guglielmo Marconi, an Italian inventor. In 1931, he came up with a way to light up the statue by sending a radio signal all the way from Italy.

The statue is made of concrete but covered in thousands of soapstone tiles. The construction workers sometimes wrote hidden messages to their family and friends on the back of the soapstone tiles.

A statue with a heart? Yes — *Christ the Redeemer* has a carved heart 1.3 m (4.3 ft) tall. That means the heart alone might be taller than you are!

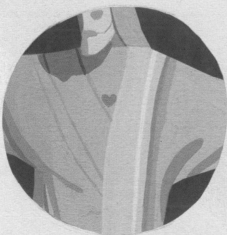

Pack Your Bag

- A swimsuit, sandals and sunscreen. After visiting Mount Corcovado, go for a swim at the beach!

- A ribbon, called a "fita of Bonfim." Named after Brazil's famous Catholic church, these ribbons are tied to the wrist with three knots. Each knot represents a wish. When the ribbon falls off, it's said that the wishes come true.

Wow!

The statue's right hand points to south Rio, and its left hand points to the north part of the city. Because it is so tall, the statue is regularly struck by lightning, which damages the concrete and soapstone tile fingers. Brave restoration workers climb the statue to repair the damage.

Tell Me a Story

Rio de Janeiro is such a beautiful place that it's easy for its Christian residents to imagine God's hand in its creation. Not only is there an enormous bay with clean white beaches (Guanabara Bay), but there is also a rainforest at the foot of Mount Corcovado. It only seems natural to have a monument there to unite the city at its highest point of 710 m (2,329 ft). To raise money to build this monument, Brazilian leaders in the Catholic church asked their followers to donate during "Monument Week." Volunteers collected money and asked people to sign a petition to the Brazilian president. They gathered over 20,000 signatures! Then they chose people to design the monument: engineer Heitor da Silva Costa, artist Carlos Oswald and sculptor Paul Landowski. Their image of Christ has open arms, as if he is welcoming everyone to Brazil with love.

Meet Mount Corcovado

Christ the Redeemer is so striking because of the natural beauty all around it. Its dramatic backdrop includes the sky and Tijuca Forest, the rainforest at the heart of Rio that is also a national park. On your way to see the statue, visit the Cascatinha Taunay Waterfall inside the forest. Notice the many animals all around: armadillos, opossums, hummingbirds, iguanas and more! Once you're at the top of Corcovado, take in the whole view of Rio from the beaches to the bay.

The Word to Know

In Portuguese, **Rio de Janeiro** means "river of January." Portuguese colonizers first arrived at Guanabara Bay in January more than 500 years ago, meeting people of several Indigenous nations including the Tupi, Puri, Botocudo and Maxakalí.

Look Up Close

The engineer Heitor da Silva Costa imagined *Christ the Redeemer* facing the sun every morning. As the sun rose, he thought, it would touch the statue's head first and create a bright halo. Da Silva Costa was inspired by the Brazilian sculptor Aleijadinho, who had used pale, long-lasting soapstone in his work. He worked with sculptors in France to create the head and hands, then sent them to Rio to join the rest of the statue.

Stonehenge (ENGLAND)

A calendar based on planets and stars? A sacred place to show respect to the people who lived and died before us? Or the work of a wizard who moved these stones here from far away? You can imagine all kinds of explanations when you explore the 5,000 years of history behind Stonehenge. There are many myths and legends associated with this famous stone circle, and archaeologists have done plenty of work to develop their own theories. In fact, based on their studies, we know that several different monuments were built, moved and changed in this same place between 3000 and 1600 BCE. Look carefully at the "hanging stones" (that's what we think "Stonehenge" means in Old English) and see what more you can find.

Enter and Be Amazed

Moving and raising these massive boulders was an incredible task! It probably took more than a hundred people to get them into place using ropes and levers. The largest stones weigh about 22.7 tonnes (25 tons), as much as five elephants.

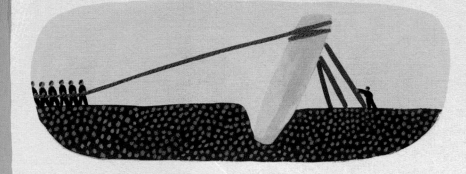

Take a closer look! On one of the stones near the entrance, you can see a mark that looks like a footprint. According to legend, the devil got angry at a monk and threw a stone at him, which hit his foot. That is why it is called the Heel Stone.

Inside the outer circle of the largest stones, you will see smaller rocks called "bluestones," because they look blue when they get wet.

In the middle of the circle stands the Altar Stone, about 5 m (16 ft) long. It lies on its side now, but some people think it originally stood upright like the other stones.

Pack Your Bag

- A collection of English and Welsh legends about the land of Stonehenge.

- Clay and a round, green rug. With these, you can make your own model of the stone circle.

The Word to Know

There are other stone circles, but Stonehenge is the only one with horizontal (sideways) stones on top of vertical (upright) stones. These horizontal stones are known as **lintels**. Inside the circle, Stonehenge originally had five pairs of uprights, each with a lintel. This formation of three stones is called a trilithon, which is Greek for "three stones."

Tell Me a Story

One legend says that these huge stones were carried by giants. It's easy to understand why — who else could have moved them so far? By studying the types of rock, archaeologists have learned that the biggest stones come from 25 km (15 mi) away and the bluestones come from the Preseli Hills in Wales, more than 250 km (155 mi) away! For people in the Middle Ages (between 500 and 1500 CE), it was natural to imagine giants or magic. They used their own medieval legends of the famous wizard Merlin to explain the mysteries of Stonehenge. Merlin, they said, brought the stones from a giants' stone circle in Ireland. In reality, groups of people might have pulled the stones over land on a wooden sledge and sailed them on rafts over water.

Meet the Druids

We used to think the builders of Stonehenge were people called Druids, a group of priests, teachers and judges in ancient Britain. Then, scientists studied the monument using radiocarbon dating, a process that can measure the age of rocks. They learned that it was actually built 2,000 years before the Druids existed! Modern-day Druids still gather at Stonehenge to celebrate the summer solstice, the longest day of the year.

Look Up Close

There's no stone circle more mysterious than Stonehenge. If you could look at it from above, you would see a round ditch almost like a moat that surrounds all of the stones. Just inside the ditch are 56 holes in the ground, where the bluestones first stood. The heaviest outside stones are called the Sarsen stones, a nickname that comes from the medieval word "Saracen," meaning anything that wasn't Christian. Then come the bluestones and the five trilithons. In the middle are the Altar Stone and more bluestones.

Wow!

Some people think Stonehenge was built to work like a calendar, helping people make calculations from the sun and moon. The stones are positioned to mark the rising sun at midsummer and the setting of the sun at midwinter. Even today, if you go to Stonehenge in the very middle of the summer, you can see the sun rise above the Heel Stone. In the middle of winter, you can see the sun setting through the stones.

Angkor Wat (CAMBODIA)

Angkor Wat, a majestic temple found in Cambodia, is one of the most sacred places in all of southeast Asia. Meaning "City of Temples," it is part of a giant group of buildings that was hidden from view for centuries by the thick, surrounding jungle. The sandstone walls of the temple feature carvings of gods and goddesses, along with religious scenes such as the creation of the world. Angkor Wat was originally a holy place in the Hindu religion but is now considered to be Buddhist.

Enter and Be Amazed

What's the most fun way to travel as you explore here? On board a tuk-tuk, a three-wheeled Cambodian taxi.

Make a second stop at the Angkor Thom complex, one of the most fascinating temples of Angkor. The upper terrace has towers made up of 200 giant carved stone faces, whose eyes seem to follow you wherever you go!

Return to Angkor Wat and admire the wall sculptures that represent mysterious goddess dancers, each one slightly different from the others.

Angkor Wat's five towers represent the five peaks of Mount Meru, a holy mountain in both the Hindu and Buddhist religions. Mount Meru is considered the house of the Hindu gods and the Buddhist focus of the spiritual universe.

Wow!

From above, Angkor Wat looks like any other building with walls and hallways and doors. Yet, there is something magical about this place. To get to Angkor Wat, you must travel along a path known as the "rainbow bridge." Along the way, learn tales about the struggles between gods, demons and the seven-headed serpents known as the Naga.

Pack Your Bag

- Sunscreen, bug spray and a raincoat. Prepare for the changeable weather.
- A krama, which is a checkered Cambodian scarf that wraps around your head but can be used in all sorts of ways.

Tell Me a Story

According to Cambodian legend, thousands of years ago, the seven-headed Naga serpents lived in a kingdom in the Pacific Ocean. An Indian prince, Preah Thaong, fell in love with the daughter of the King of the Nagas and asked to marry her. The king, a nine-headed serpent, ordered his subjects to drink the water that covered those lands to make a kingdom for the newlyweds. It became the land of Khmer, now called Cambodia.

Look Up Close

Angkor Wat lives in harmony with the nature around it. The temple walls are covered in moss and surrounded by bushes and tall, hundred-year-old trees. Their roots have grown over the stones so thoroughly, they have almost become part of the building itself.

Meet Suryavarman II

The most powerful leader of the Khmer empire was named Suryavarman II. He was fearless. It is said that he won the throne by jumping onto his uncle's elephant and killing his uncle. His most important creation was Angkor Wat. It was built in only 30 years and completed in the year 1150 CE. You can see an image of Suryavarman II at Angkor Wat today. A wall sculpture shows him seated on a great elephant as he leads his army.

The Word to Know

The **Khmer** are the ancient ancestors of the Cambodians, the people who now live on the land of the Khmer empire. The Khmer language, art and culture have been preserved for over 600 years.

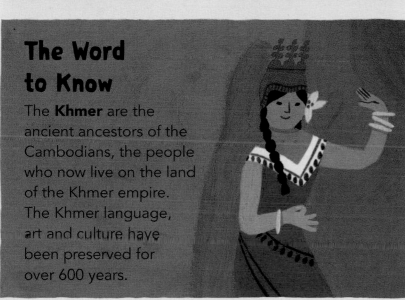

Sydney Opera House (AUSTRALIA)

Sydney Opera House sits on a strip of land that juts out over the ocean. The land is called Bennelong Point after Woollarawarre Bennelong, one of the Indigenous Eora people who lived there before the British colonized Australia. The Opera House is one of the most impressive buildings for performing arts (music, drama and dance) in the world. It is as much a part of Australian identity as the kangaroo, the koala and the surfboard. It contains about 1,000 rooms, where all kinds of events take place 363 days of the year. What are you hoping to find inside?

Enter and Be Amazed

Make sure you stand back to get the best view. The ocean is not only a pretty backdrop here — the building uses seawater to power its heating and air-conditioning.

Let's look at the numbers: It took two years to design the building, plus fourteen years of work costing 102 million Australian dollars to complete it. There are about 1,000 rooms inside, including six restaurants!

It's your lucky day! Imagine sitting in one of the 1,500 seats in the Concert Hall and listening to the Sydney Symphony Orchestra play Beethoven's Ninth Symphony, just like they did at the Opera House's opening in 1973.

Inside, there are ballets, concerts, even conferences — and you can see shows outside, too. The Opera House's many sail-shaped roofs light up during festivals like Lunar New Year.

The Word to Know

Australians often refer to themselves as **Aussies**. One of the most famous symbols of this country is the cuddly koala! You might even find a toy koala to take home with you.

Pack Your Bag

- A pair of shorts and dressy clothes. During the day, hang around in the rooms of the Opera House in shorts, but at night, put on something fancier to enjoy a concert or a ballet.

- A boomerang, the wooden hunting weapon of the Aboriginal peoples who were the first to live in Australia. Throw it and try to make it come back into your hands.

Meet Jørn Utzon

Jørn Utzon, who designed the Sydney Opera House, was born in Copenhagen, a Danish city near the water. His father designed ships. Utzon was inspired by the Maya pyramids at Chichén Itzá. With their stepped platforms as tall as the jungle, people could climb to the top of the pyramids and be in another world. Jørn wanted people to feel the same way at the Opera House, looking out at the water. In 2007, the Opera House was named a World Heritage Site, and Jørn became one of only two living architects to see their work receive that award.

Tell Me a Story

How did architect Jørn Utzon design fourteen beautiful curves that also form a sturdy roof? Jørn demonstrated his plan on television by peeling an orange. The roof's shapes, he showed, could be like the peel. Together, they formed a perfect sphere, but separated, each one looked like a sail. These sails reflect the light off the ocean around them and give the Opera House its high ceilings.

Look Up Close

Stretched out over Bennelong Point, the site of this giant building is so enormous it could fit seven planes side by side. From the outside, the most incredible part is the roof of sails: 2,200 concrete "ribs" connect and support these astounding roof structures. More than a million roof tiles, made in Sweden, cover the surface of the sails and shine as they reflect light.

Wow!

Amazing to admire from the outside, the Opera House also takes your breath away when you are inside. Most impressive is the Concert Hall, which is lined from floor to ceiling with wood from Australian trees. You can sit in one of the seats and look up at the high, cathedral-like ceilings. In front of you is the largest mechanical pipe organ in the world. Its sound is naturally made louder by the way the hall is built.

This book uses the abbreviations **BCE** and **CE** to describe dates in history. They stand for "before common era" and "common era." You might have also heard of the terms **BC** and **AD**, which stand for Latin words meaning "before and after the birth of Jesus Christ." The "common era" is also measured before and after this event.

Barefoot Books would like to thank
**Alexandra Apito; Bryan Apito, RA;
Professor Adrian Carter; Dr. Mary Jane Cuyler;
Dr. Ebba Koch; William Lindesay;
Dr. Carl P. Lipo; Dr. Peter Der Manuelian;
Professor Mike Parker Pearson; and Dr. Sarah Scher**
for their help in the editing of this book.

Barefoot Books
23 Bradford Street, 2nd Floor
Concord, MA 01742

Barefoot Books
29/30 Fitzroy Square
London, W1T 6LQ

Original Italian edition: © Dalcò Edizioni Srl
Via Mazzini 6 – 43121 Parma, Italy
www.dalcoedizioni.it
Text by Miralda Colombo
Illustrations by Beatrice Cerocchi

Translation copyright © 2020 by Barefoot Books
The moral rights of Miralda Colombo and
Beatrice Cerocchi have been asserted

First published in United States of America by
Barefoot Books, Inc and in Great Britain by
Barefoot Books, Ltd in 2020
All rights reserved

Graphic design by Sarah Soldano and
Lindsey Leigh, Barefoot Books
Edited by Barefoot Books
Translation support provided by Danielle Buonaiuto
Reproduction by Bright Arts, Hong Kong
Printed in China
This book was typeset in Avenir and Graphen
The illustrations were prepared in
gouache and pastels

Hardback ISBN 978-1-64686-067-8
E-book ISBN 978-1-64686-084-5

British Cataloguing-in-Publication Data: a catalogue record
for this book is available from the British Library

Library of Congress Cataloging-in-Publication Data
is available under LCCN 2020012209 (print)
and LCCN 2020012210 (e-book)

3 5 7 9 8 6 4 2

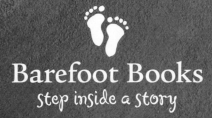

Barefoot Books
step inside a story

At Barefoot Books, we celebrate art and story that opens the hearts and minds of children from all walks of life, focusing on themes that encourage independence of spirit, enthusiasm for learning and respect for the world's diversity. The welfare of our children is dependent on the welfare of the planet, so we source paper from sustainably managed forests and constantly strive to reduce our environmental impact. Playful, beautiful and created to last a lifetime, our products combine the best of the present with the best of the past to educate our children as the caretakers of tomorrow.

www.barefootbooks.com

Miralda Colombo always has a suitcase in her hand. Making the most of her passion for seeing the world, she works as a journalist and writes about travel and cooking. She published her first book, a cookbook for children and families, after the birth of her daughter Alice. She lives in Italy with her husband and three children.

Beatrice Cerocchi studied illustration in Macerata, Italy, completed a degree in architecture at Rome Tre University and gained a master's degree in illustration from MiMaster in Milan. Her works have been featured in several magazines and picture books, and in 2018 she was selected for the illustrators exhibition at the Bologna Children's Book Fair. She lives and works in Rome.